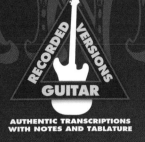

RECORDED VERSIONS
GUITAR
AUTHENTIC TRANSCRIPTIONS
WITH NOTES AND TABLATURE

ANDY McKEE

3   JOYLAND

9   BLUE LIQUID

15   AWAY

23   EVERYBODY WANTS
      TO RULE THE WORLD

30   NEVER GROW OLD

35   UPWARD MOBILITY

40   HUNTER'S MOON

46   MY LIFE AS A CPA
      (PARALLEL UNIVERSE #43)

51   LAYOVER

54   FOR NOW

Music transcriptions by Andy McKee and David Stocker

ISBN 978-1-4234-9261-0

HAL•LEONARD®
CORPORATION
7777 W. BLUEMOUND RD. P.O. BOX 13819 MILWAUKEE, WI 53213

Visit Hal Leonard Online at
www.halleonard.com

Joyland

Music by Andy McKee

Baritone Guitar tuning:
(low to high) A↓-E↓-A↓-B↓-E↓-C#↓

A

Moderately fast ♩ = 140
Fade in

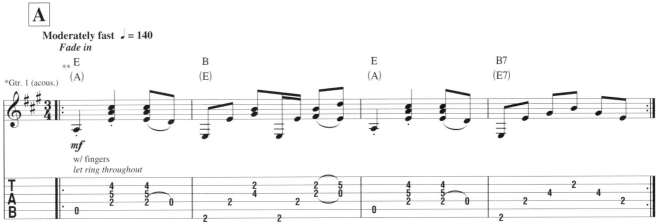

*Gtr. 1 (acous.)
**Symbols in parentheses represent chord names respective to Baritone Guitar. Symbols above represent actual sounding chords. Music sounds a perfect fourth lower than written to facilitate note reading. Chord symbols reflect overall harmony.
*Baritone Gtr.

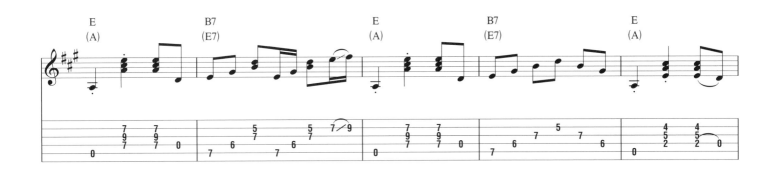

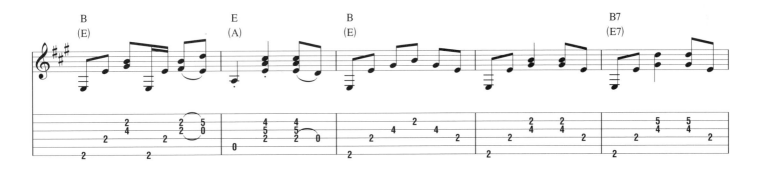

B

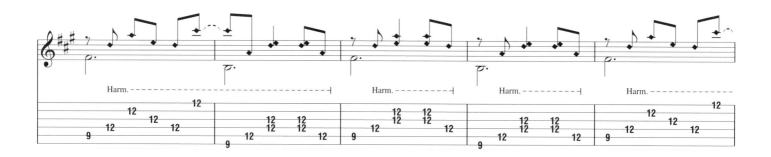

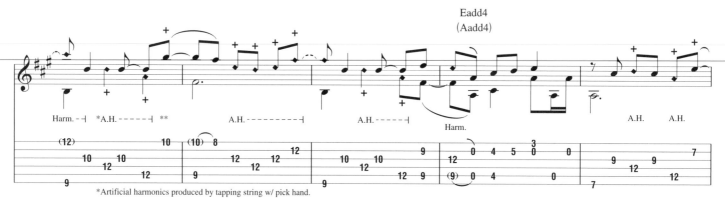

*Artificial harmonics produced by tapping string w/ pick hand.

**Fret string normally w/ fret hand and sound string by tapping w/ pick hand.

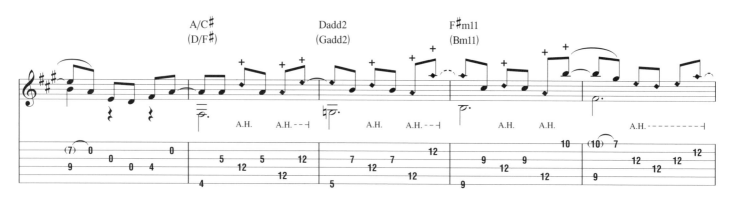

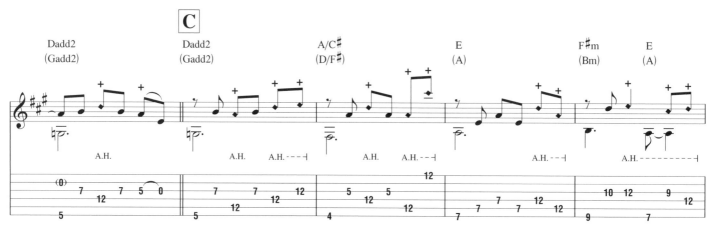

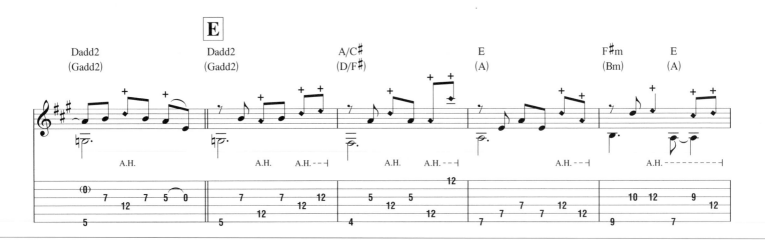

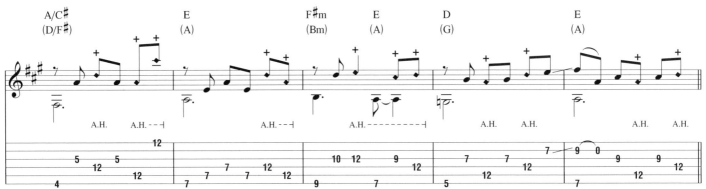

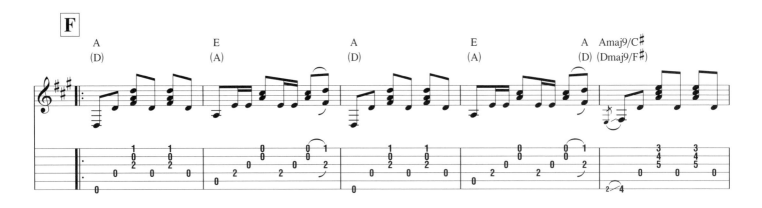

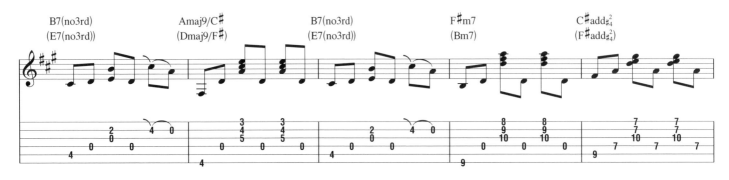

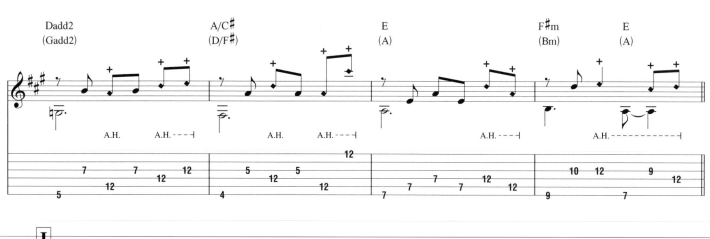

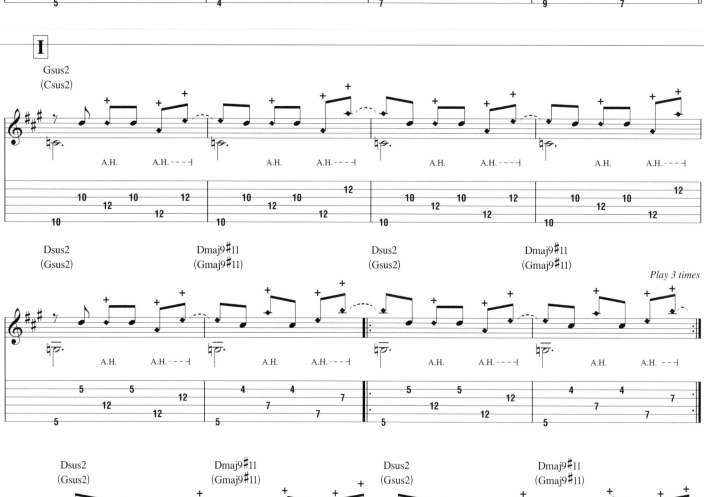

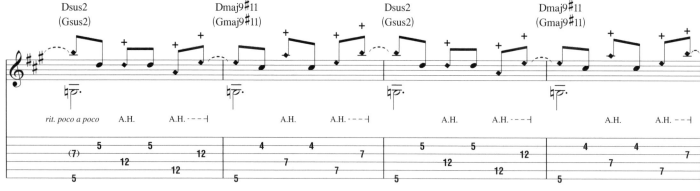

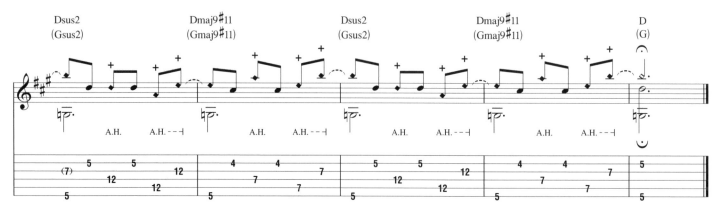

Blue Liquid

Music by Andy McKee

Baritone Guitar tuning:
(low to high) C#-E↓-F#-B-D#-F#

*Baritone Gtr. **Chord symbols reflect overall harmony.   †Slap strings with thumb of pick hand.
***Tap on the face of the guitar (lower bout for x's on beats 1 & 2, upper bout for beat 3) w/ pick-hand fingers (p = thumb, i = index, m = middle, a = ring, c = little) in the rhythm indicated.

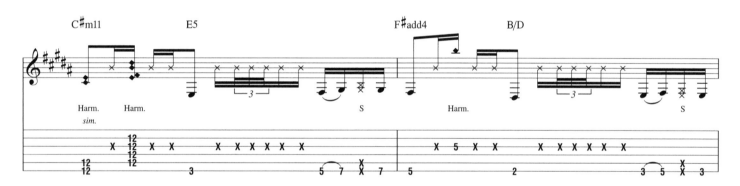

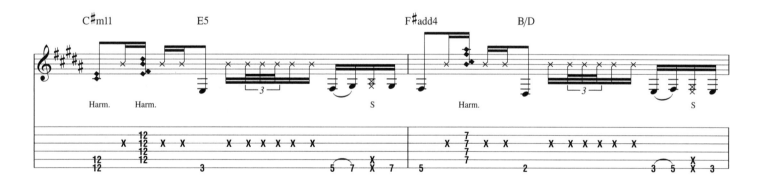

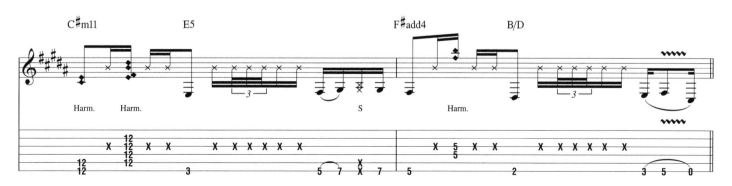

B

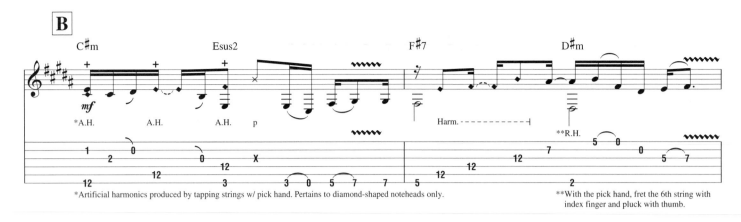

*Artificial harmonics produced by tapping strings w/ pick hand. Pertains to diamond-shaped noteheads only.

**With the pick hand, fret the 6th string with index finger and pluck with thumb.

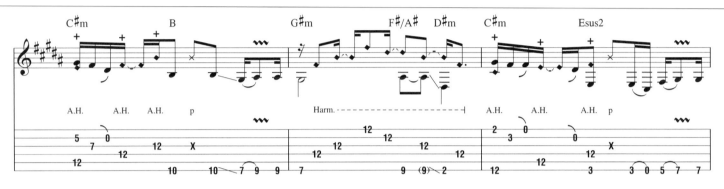

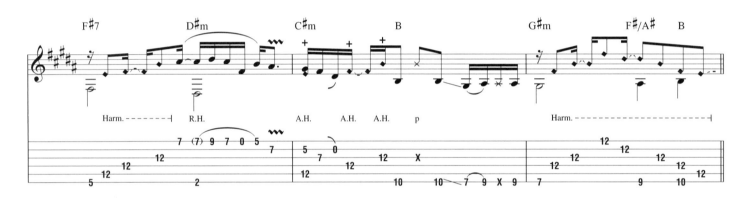

C

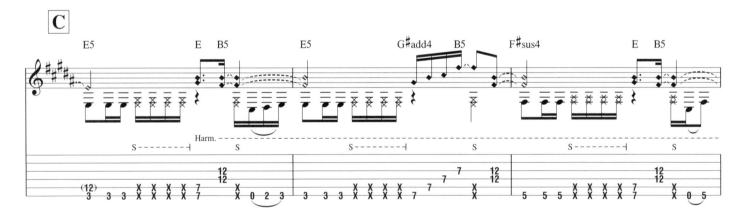

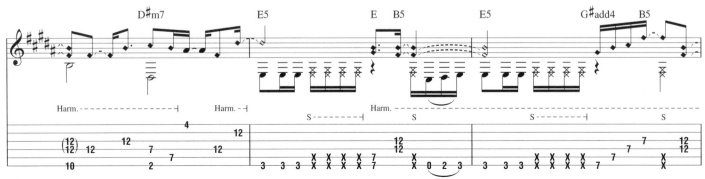

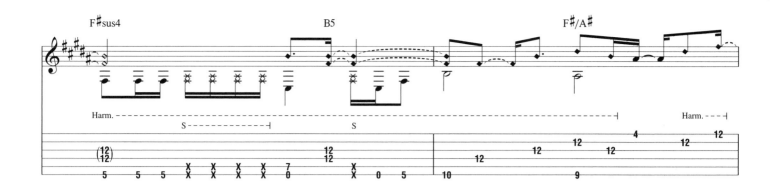

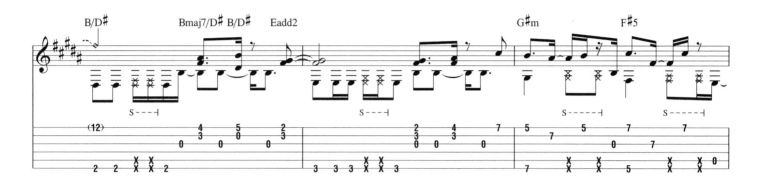

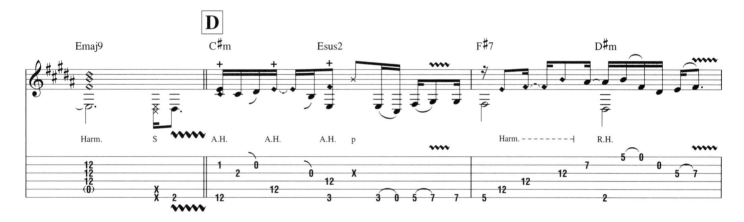

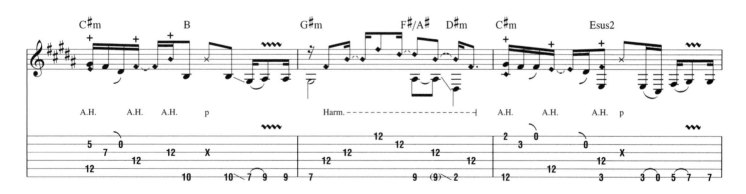

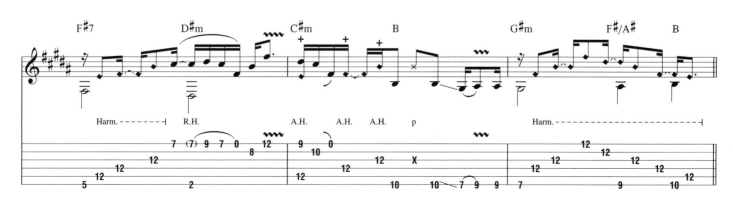

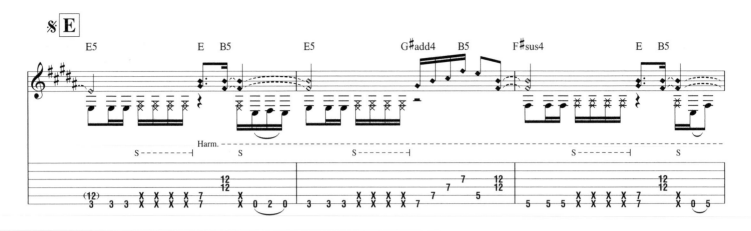

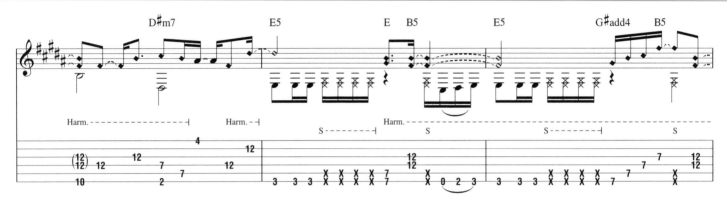

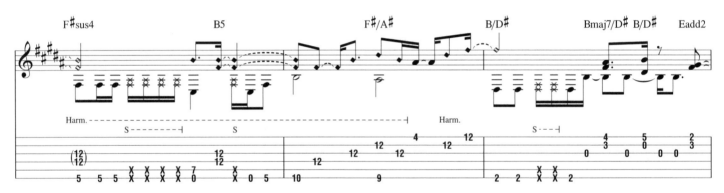

*With the pick hand, touch open strings at fret indicated and pluck with ring finger to sound harmonic. Pertains to diamond-shaped noteheads only.

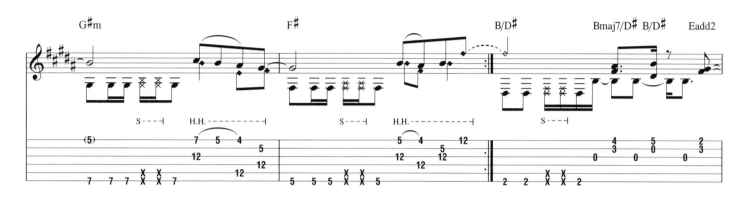

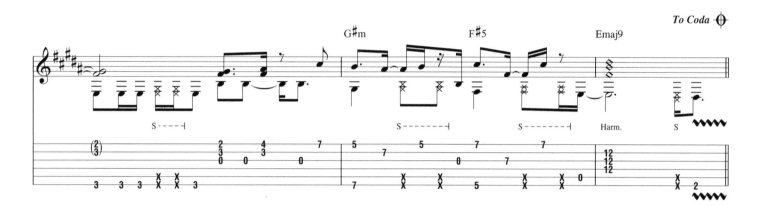

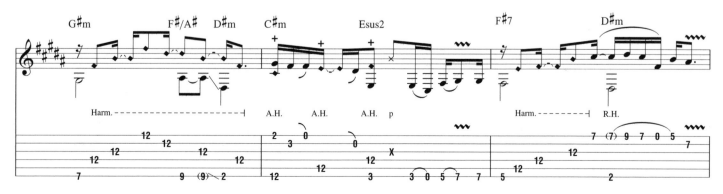

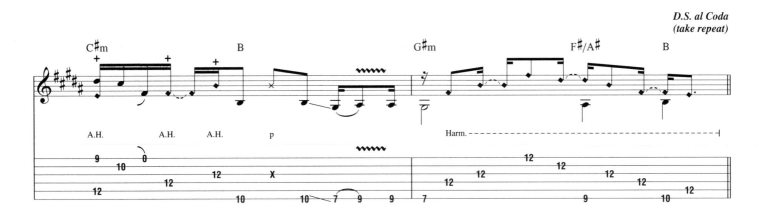

⊕ Coda

H

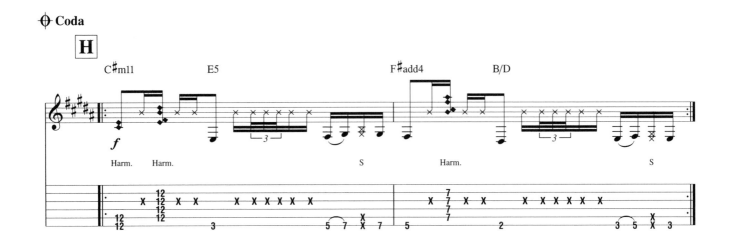

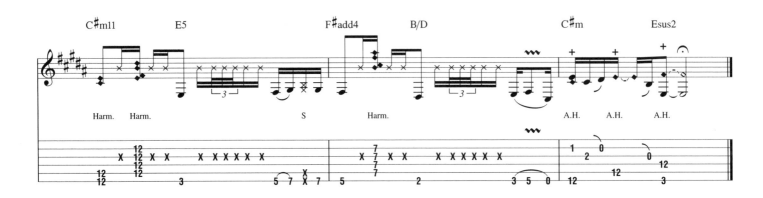

Away

Music by Andy McKee

Harp Guitar tuning:

Bass strings:
(low to high) F#-G#-A-B-C#-E
Standard strings, Partial capo II (6th - 3rd strings):
(low to high) E-B-D-G-B-E

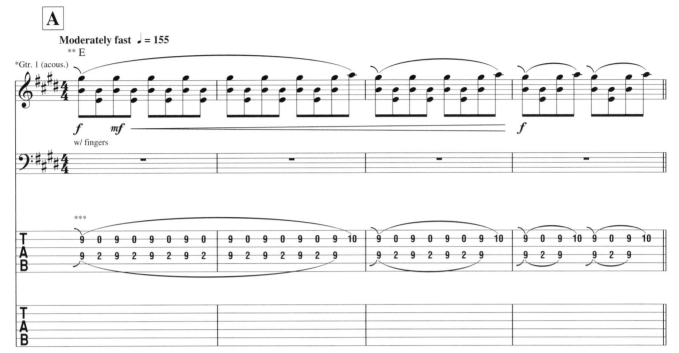

*12-str. Harp Guitar.
　　**Chord symbols reflect implied harmony.
　　***Capoed fret is "2" in tab. All tab numbers reflect actual fret positions.

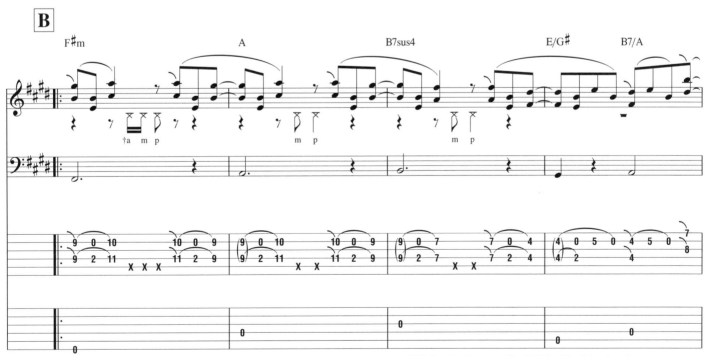

†Tap on soundboard above bass strings w/ pick-hand fingers (a = ring finger, m = middle finger), and on upper side w/ pick-hand thumb (p = thumb).

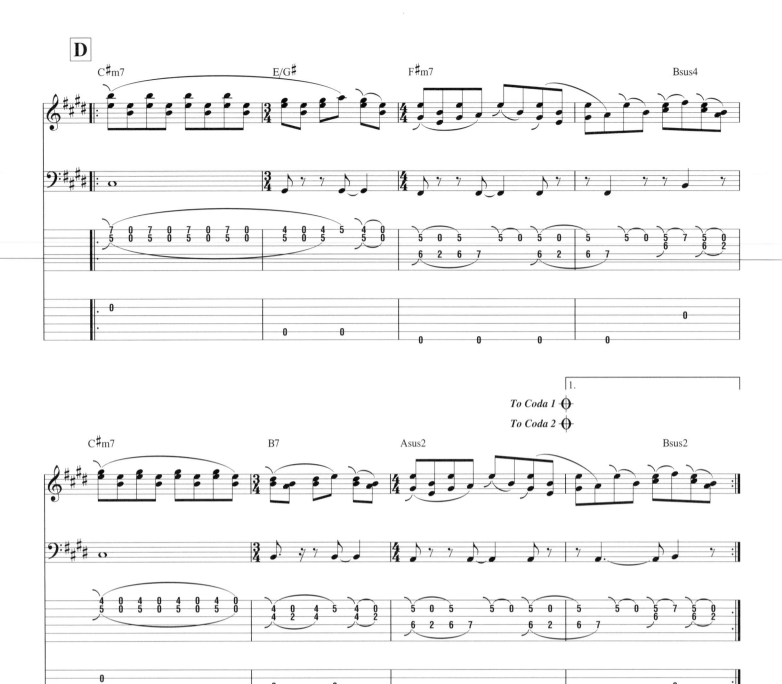

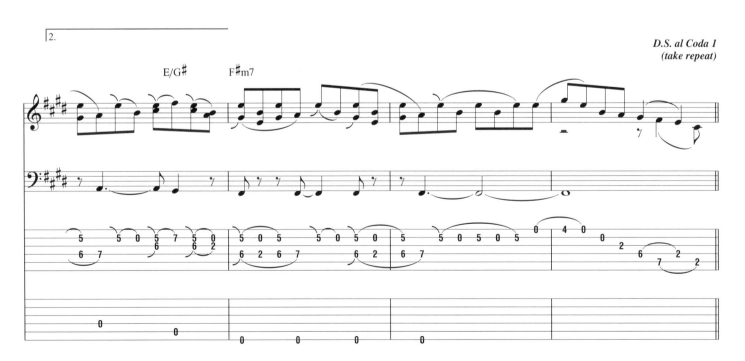

⊕ Coda 1

E

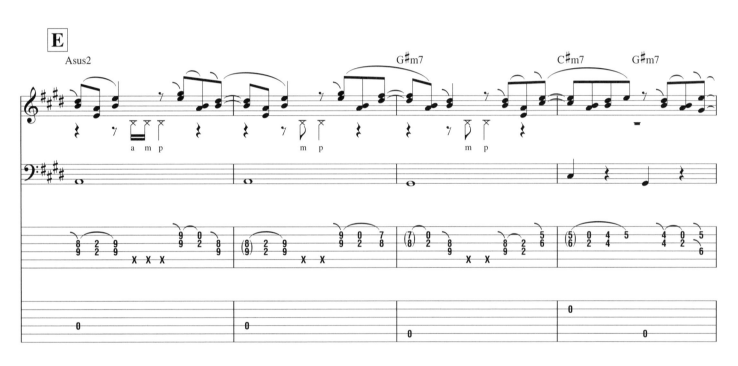

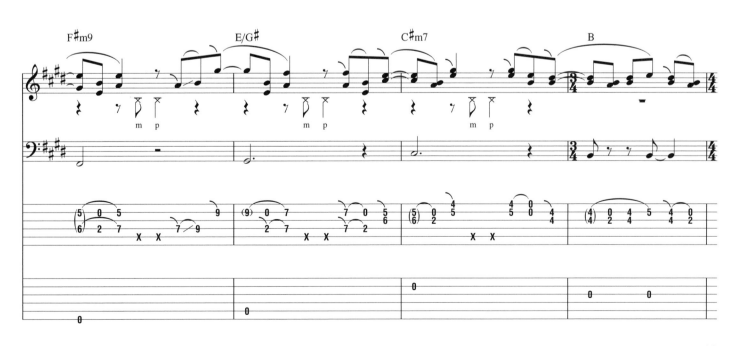

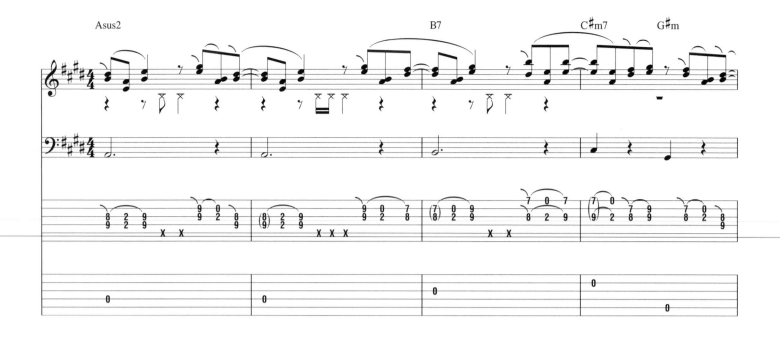

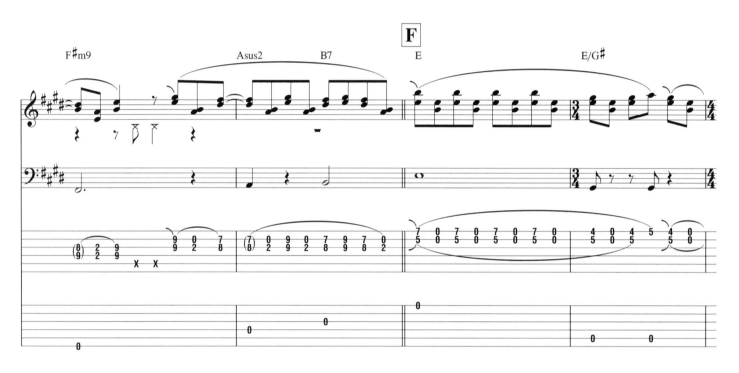

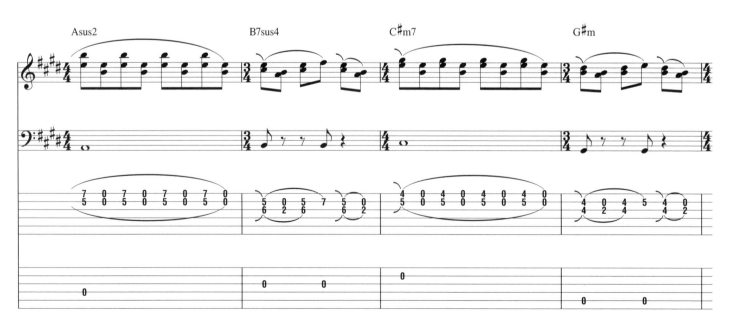

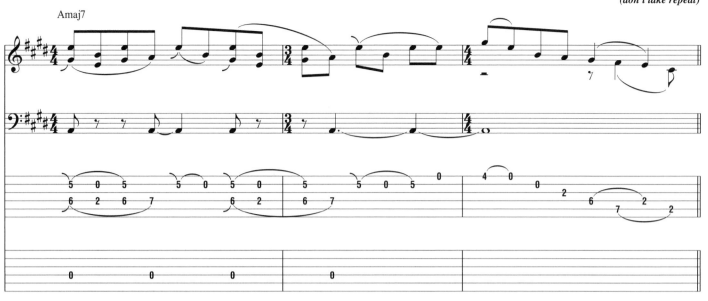

Coda 2

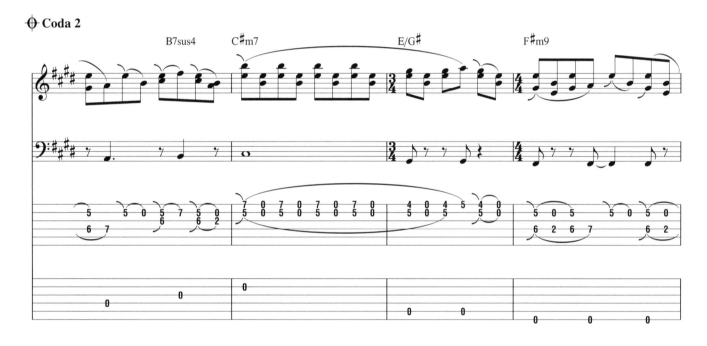

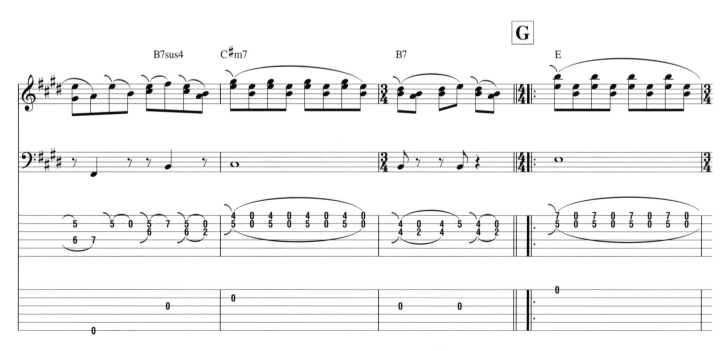

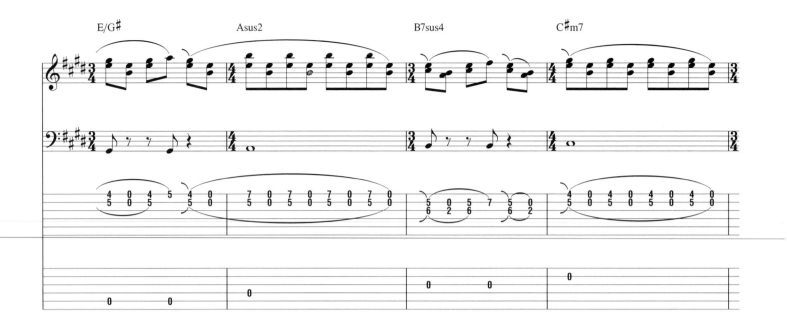

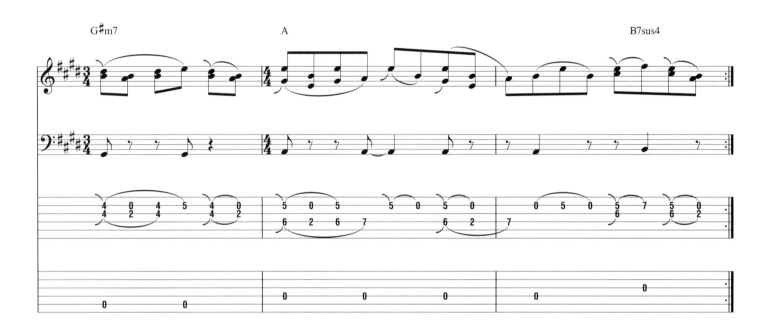

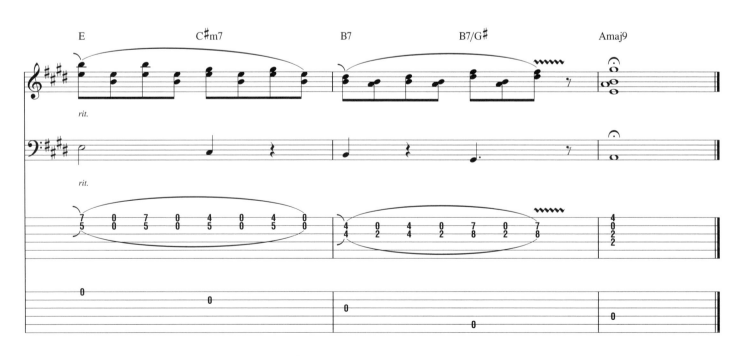

Everybody Wants to Rule the World

Words and Music by Ian Stanley, Roland Orzabal and Chris Hughes

Open D6 tuning:
(low to high) D-A-D-F♯-B-D

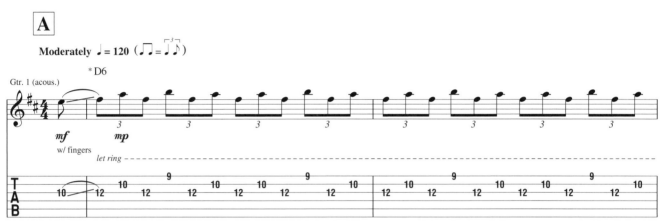

*Chord symbols reflect basic harmony.

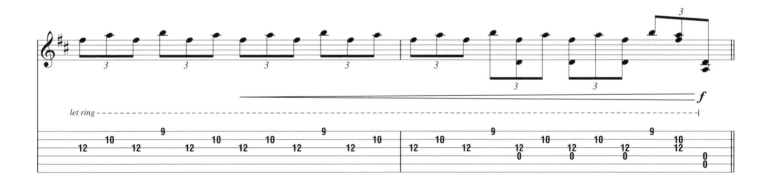

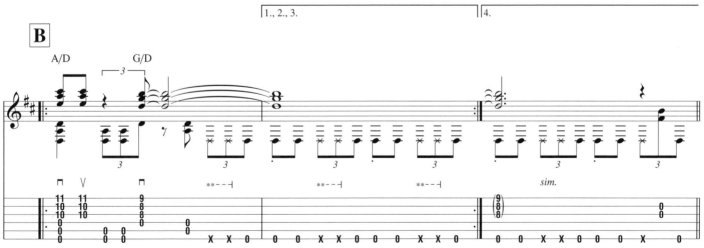

**Slap all strings w/ pick hand when low D X is written throughout.

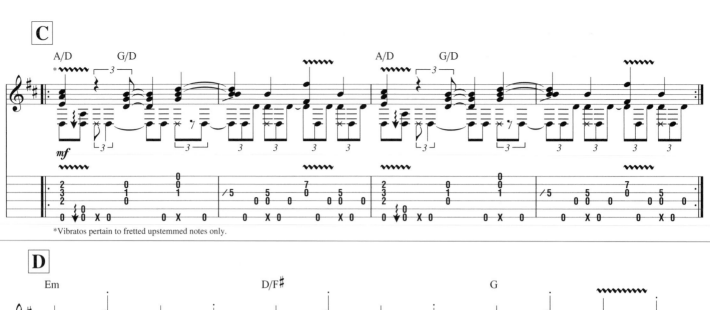

*Vibratos pertain to fretted upstemmed notes only.

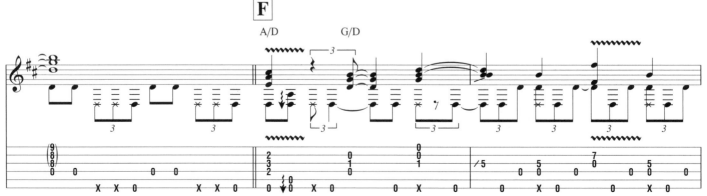

*Pull off fingers separately.

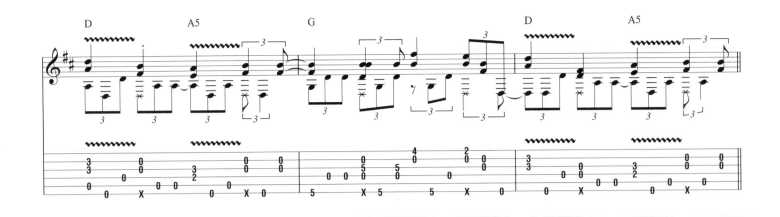

I

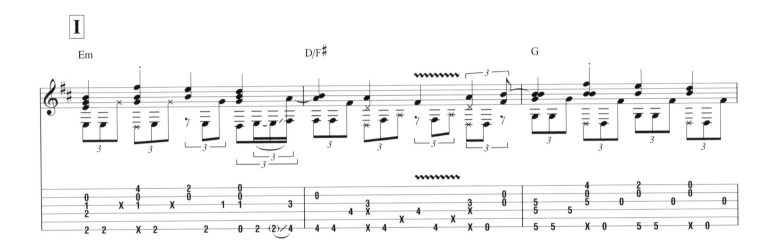

J

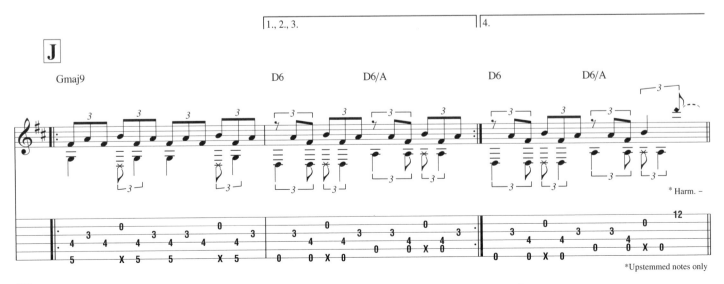

*Upstemmed notes only

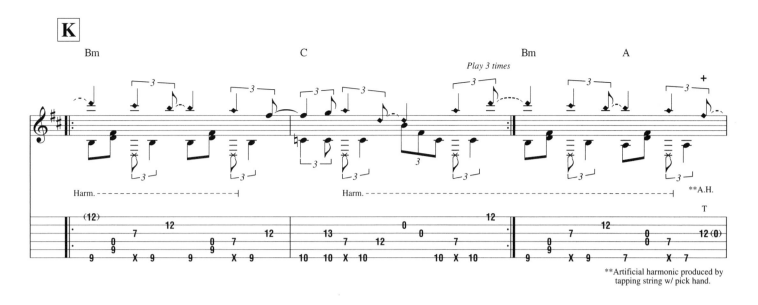

K

Bm · · · · · · · · · · C · *Play 3 times* · Bm · · · · · · · · · · A

Harm. ------------------------ | **Harm.** ------------------------ ⌐ ****A.H.**

**Artificial harmonic produced by tapping string w/ pick hand.

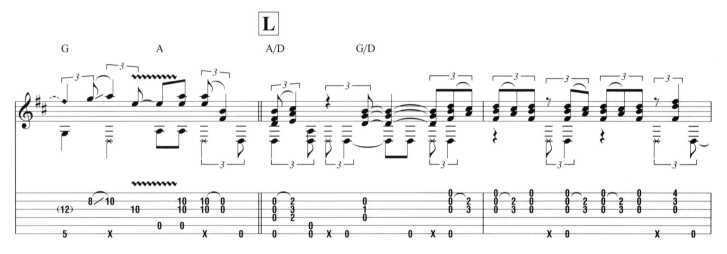

L

G · · · · · · · · · · A · · · · · · · · · · · · A/D · · · · · · · · · G/D

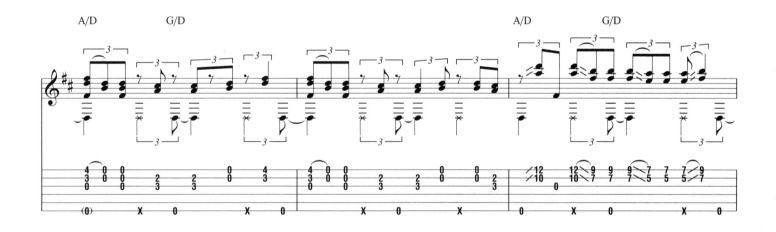

A/D · · · · · · · · · G/D · A/D · · · · · · · · · G/D

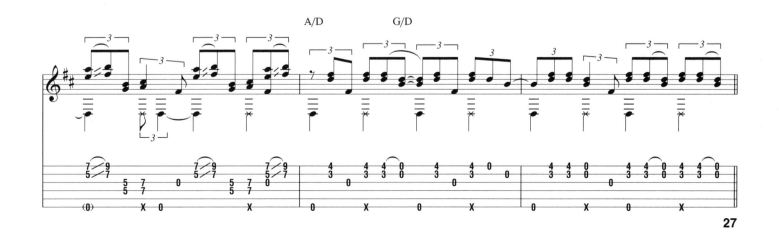

A/D · · · · · · · · · G/D

Never Grow Old

Music by Andy McKee

Tuning, Capo III:
(low to high) B♭-G-D-G-A-D

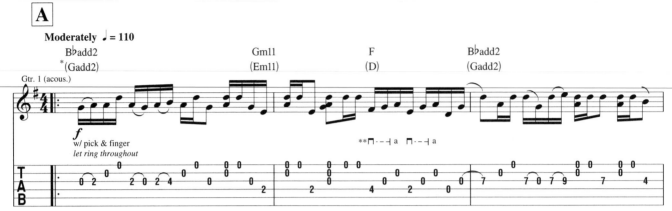

*Symbols in parentheses represent chord names respective to capoed guitar. Symbols above represent actual sounding chords. Capoed fret is "0" in tab. Chord symbols reflect overall harmony.   **a=pick-hand ring finger.

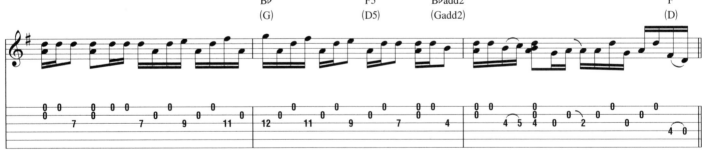

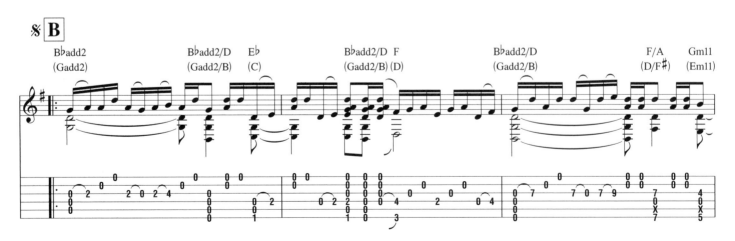

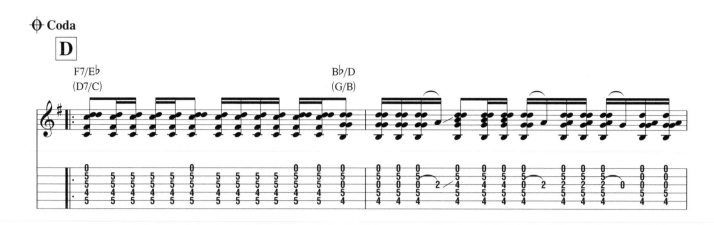

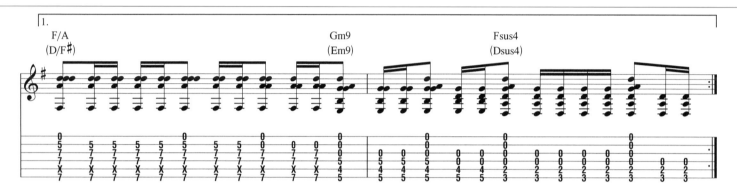

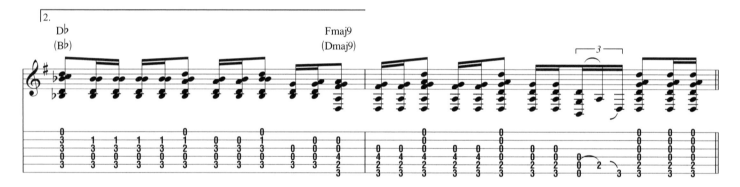

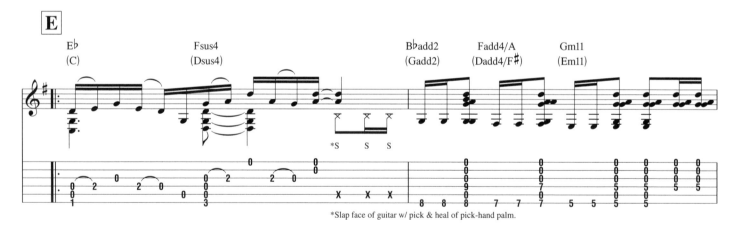

*Slap face of guitar w/ pick & heal of pick-hand palm.

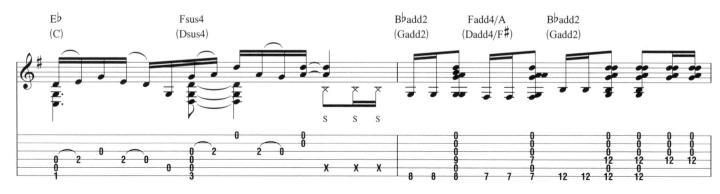

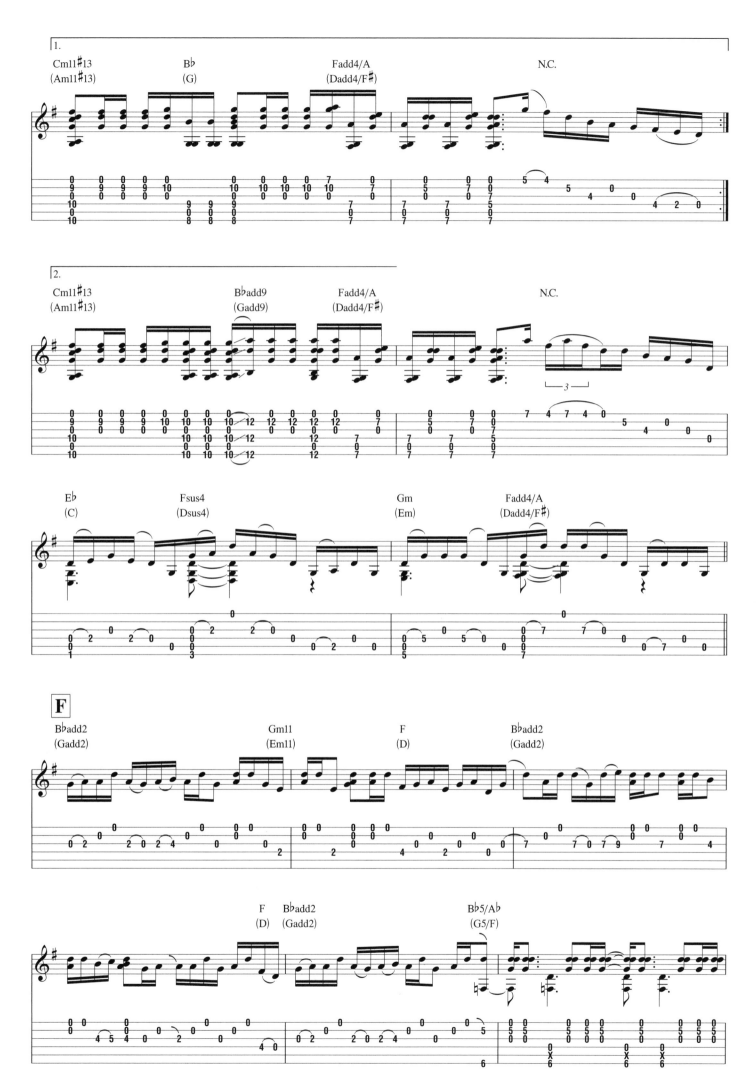

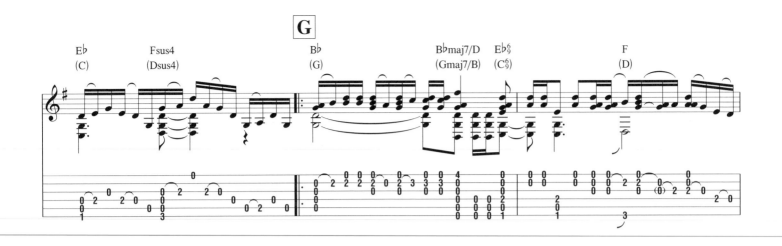

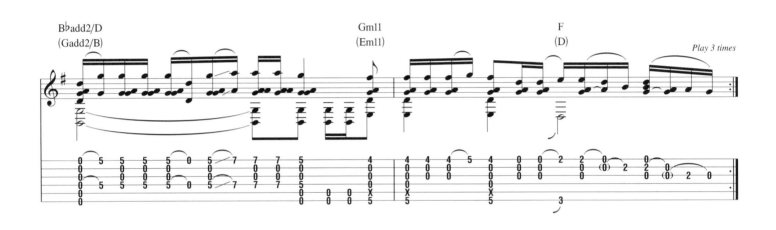

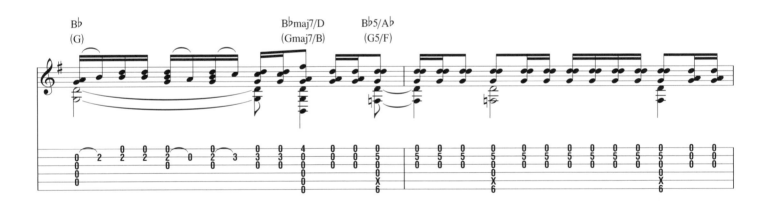

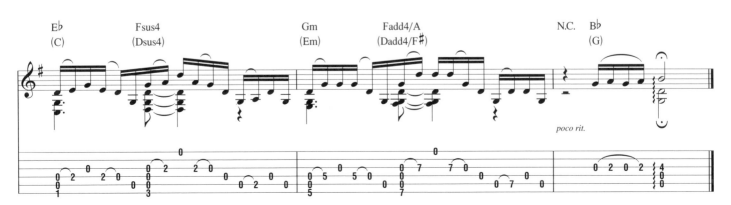

Upward Mobility

Music by Andy McKee

Tuning:
(low to high) C-G-D-G-A-D

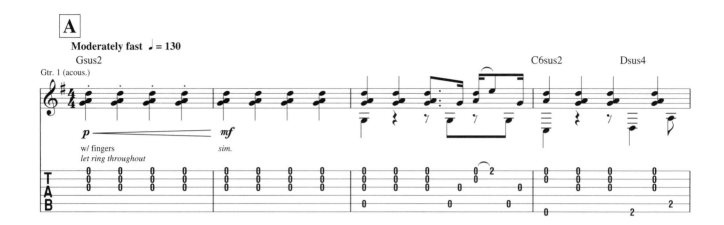

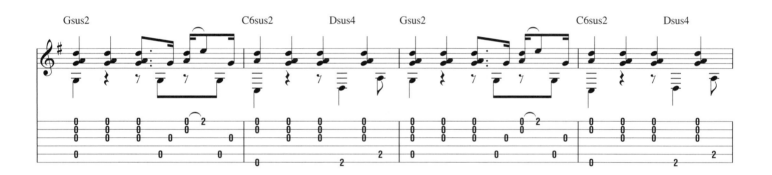

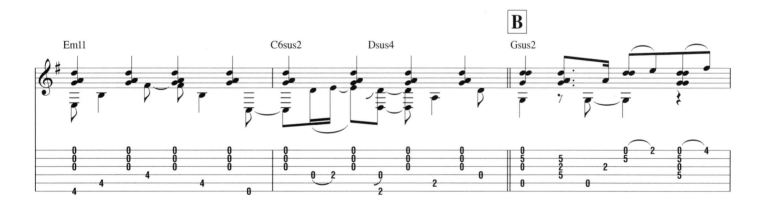

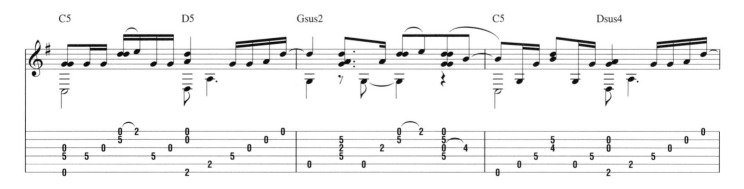

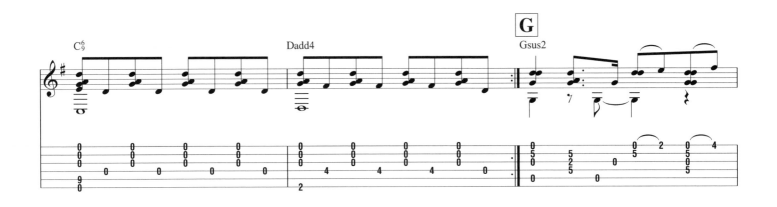

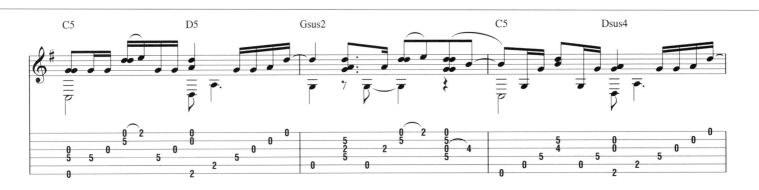

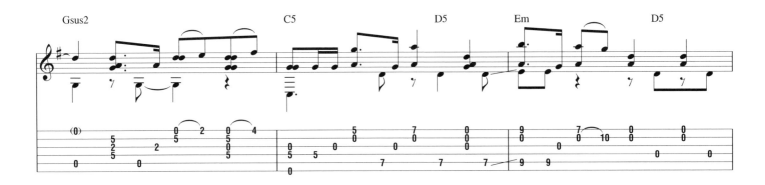

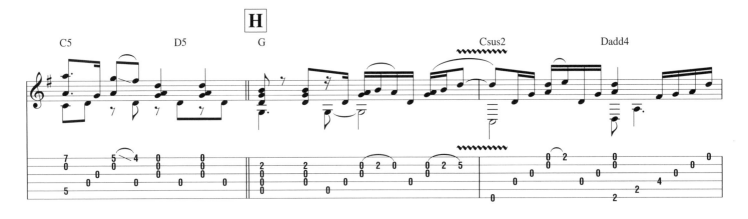

Hunter's Moon

Music by Andy McKee

Tuning:
(low to high) C-G-D-F-B♭-D

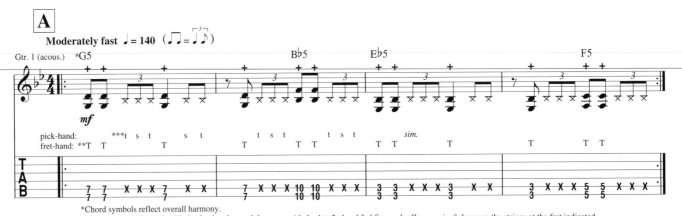

*Chord symbols reflect overall harmony.
**Reaching over the neck with the fret hand, sound the notes with the 1st, 2nd and 3rd fingers by "hammering" down on the strings at the fret indicated.
***Tap on face and bouts of guitar w/ pick-hand (s = fingers on lower bout, t = thumb on face below the bridge) and fret-hand (F = fingers on face near the fretboard,
p = palm on upper bout) in the rhythm indicated.

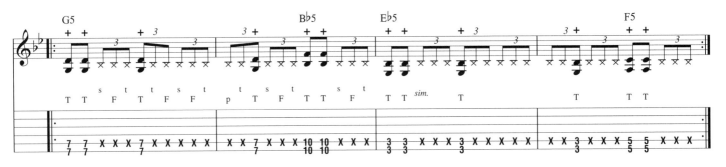

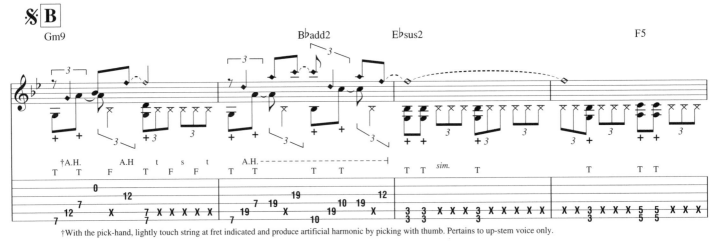

†With the pick-hand, lightly touch string at fret indicated and produce artificial harmonic by picking with thumb. Pertains to up-stem voice only.

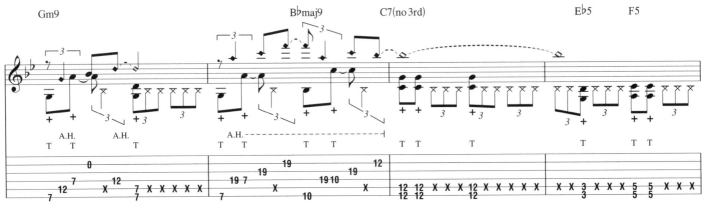

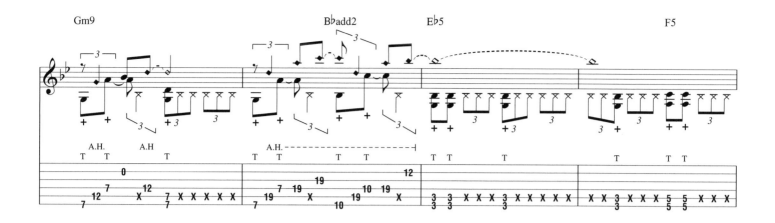

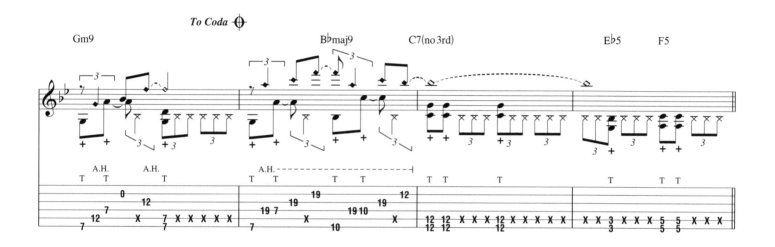

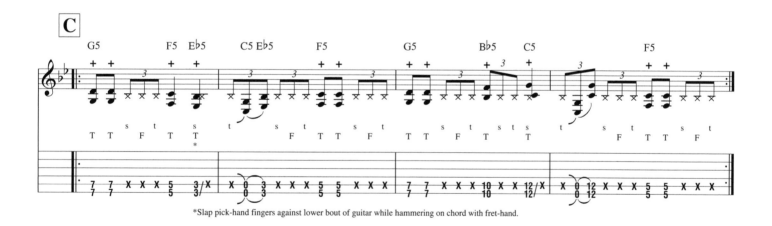

*Slap pick-hand fingers against lower bout of guitar while hammering on chord with fret-hand.

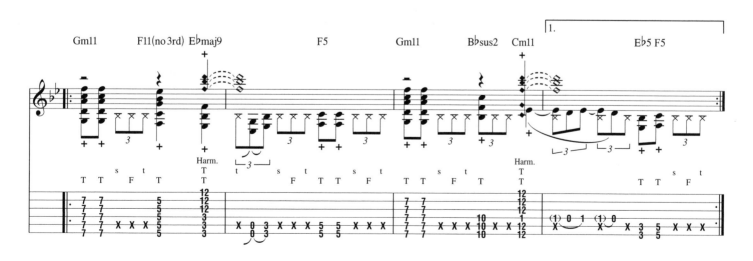

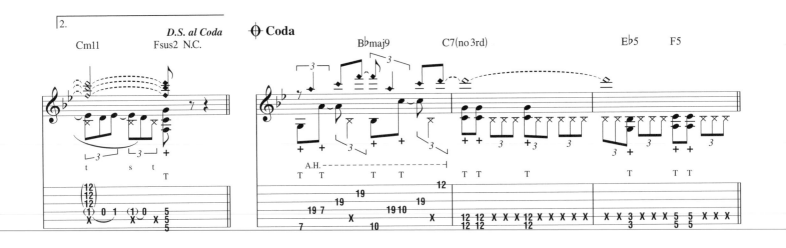

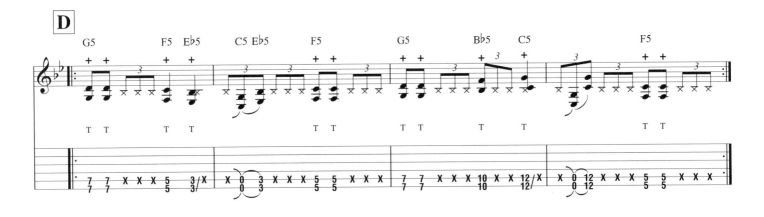

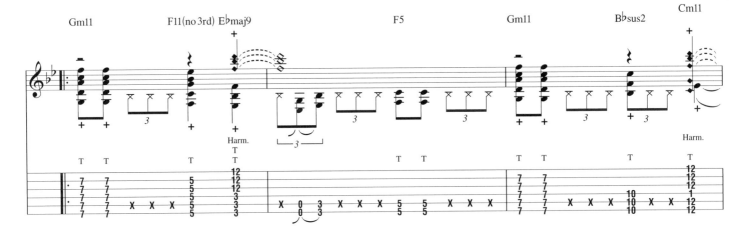

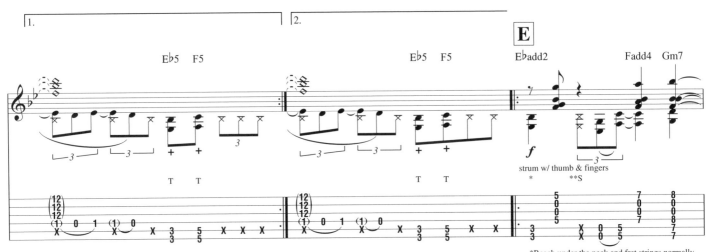

*Reach under the neck and fret strings normally.
**Slap strings w/ fingers of pick hand.

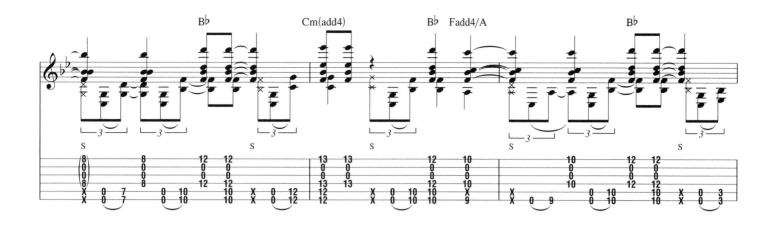

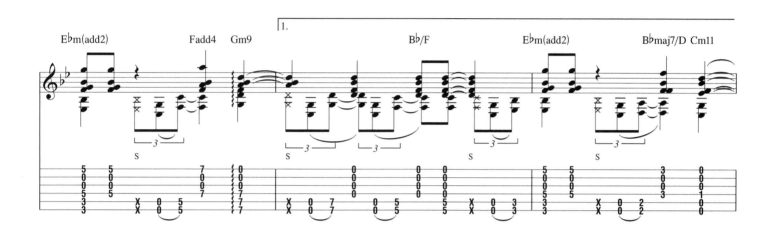

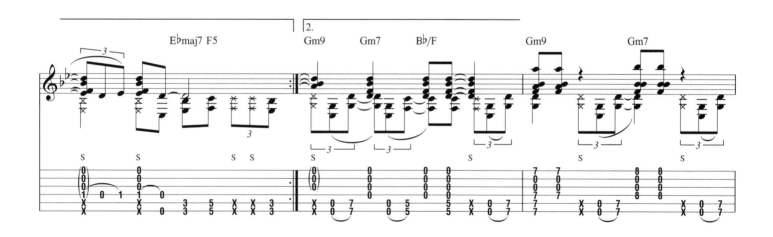

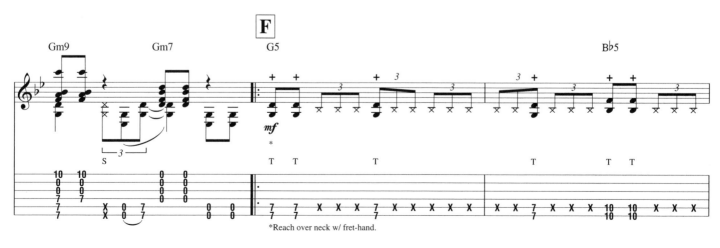

*Reach over neck w/ fret-hand.

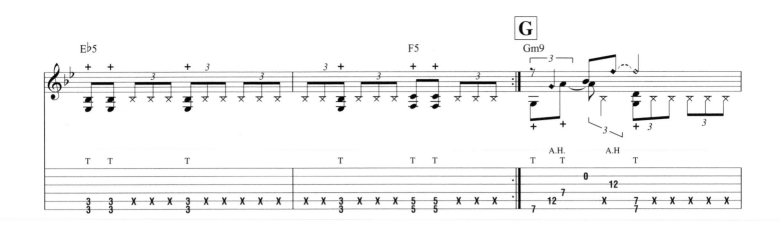

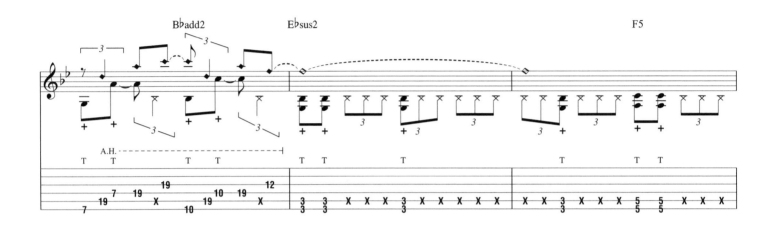

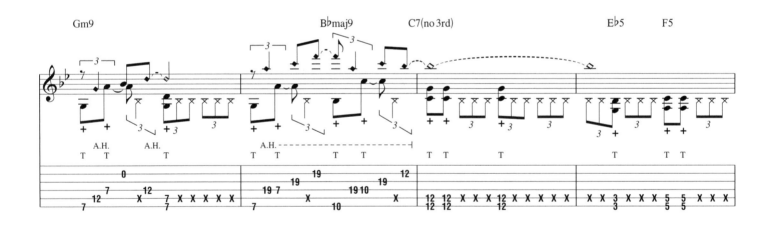

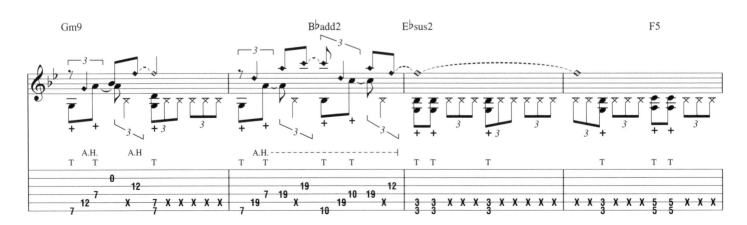

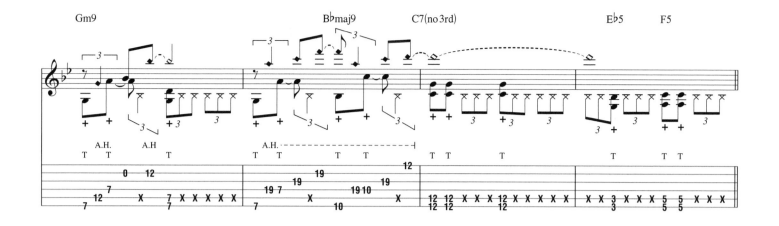

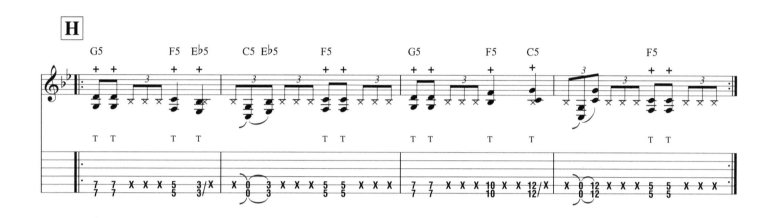

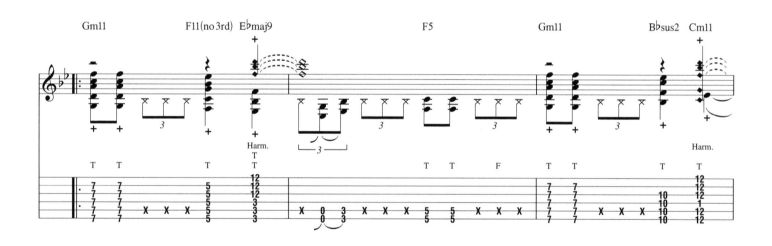

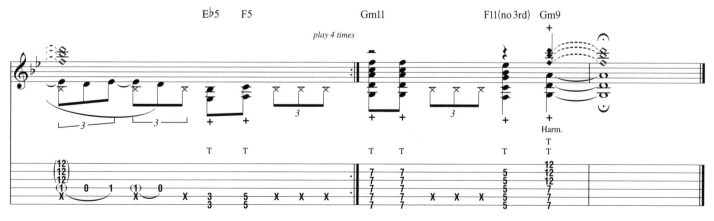

My Life as a CPA
(Parallel Universe #43)
Music by Andy McKee

Tuning, Capo III:
(low to high) D-A-D-E-A-C#

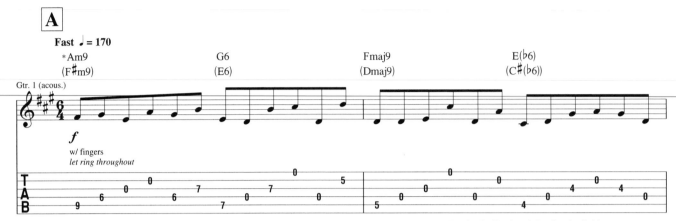

*Symbols in parenthese represent chord names respective to capoed guitar. Symbols above represent actual sounding chords. Chord symbols reflect implied harmony.
Capoed fret is "0" in tab.

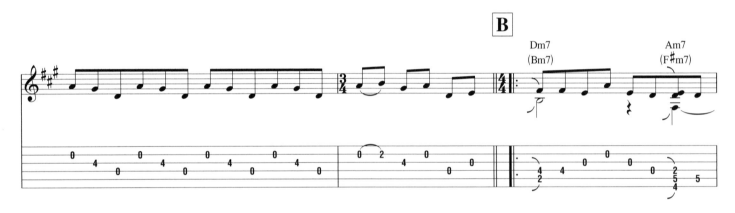

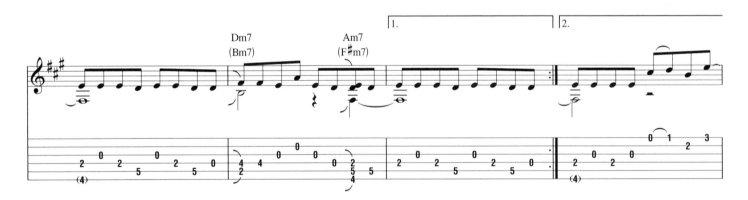

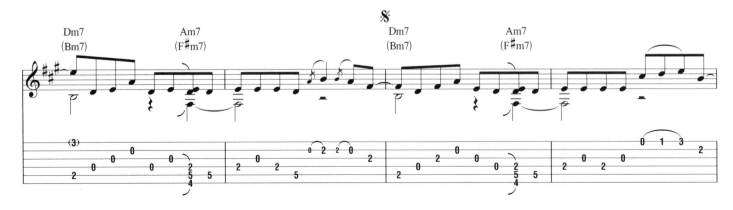

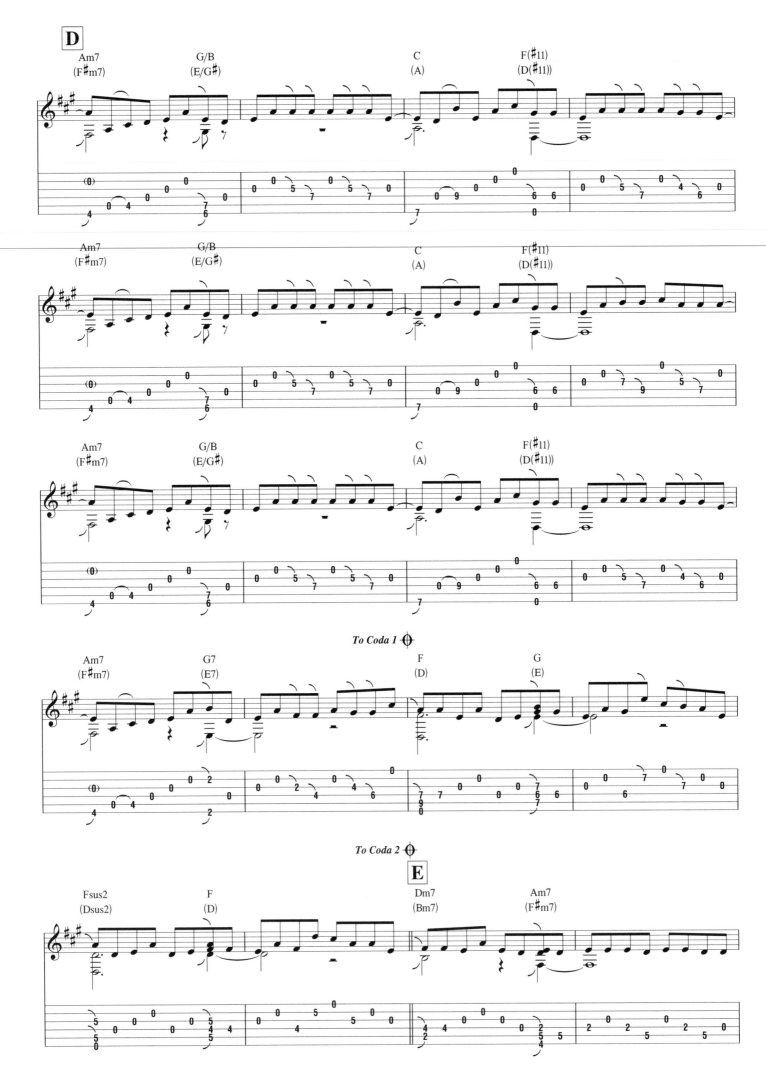

Coda 1

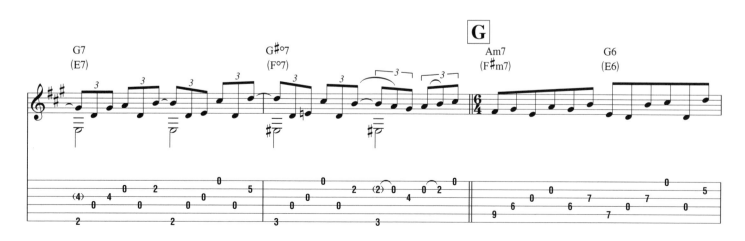

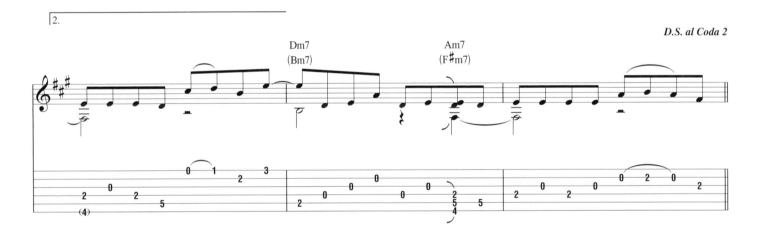

Coda 2

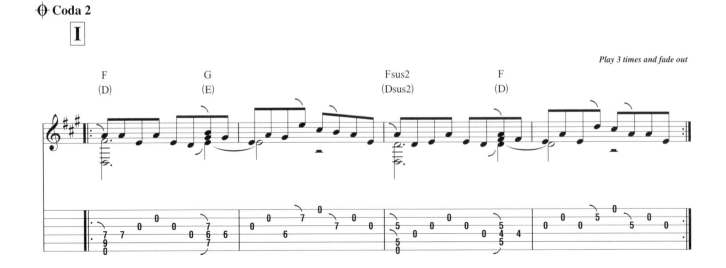

Layover

Composed by Michael Hedges

Tuning:
(low to high) D-A-C-G-C-E

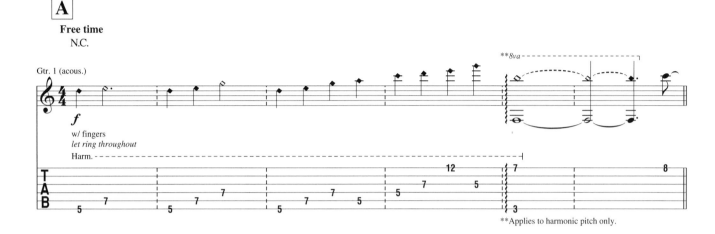

A

Free time
N.C.

Gtr. 1 (acous.)

**8va

f

w/ fingers
let ring throughout
Harm.

**Applies to harmonic pitch only.

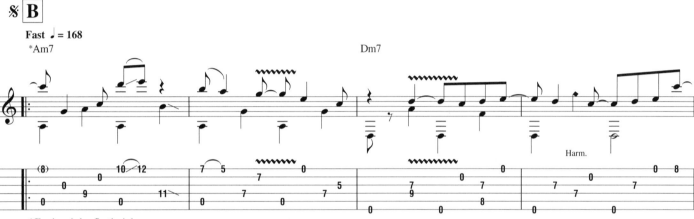

B

Fast ♩ = 168

*Am7

Dm7

*Chord symbols reflect basic harmony.

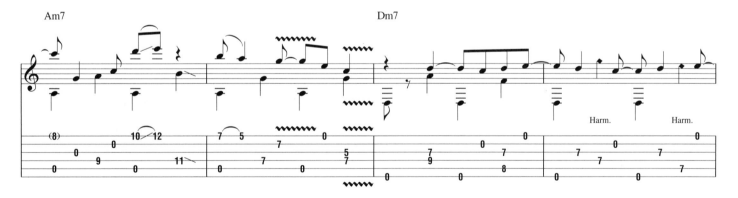

Am7

Dm7

Harm.   Harm.

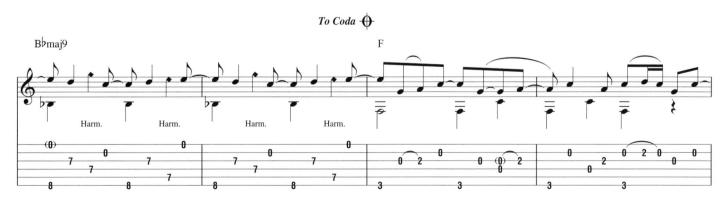

To Coda ⊕

B♭maj9

F

Harm.   Harm.   Harm.   Harm.

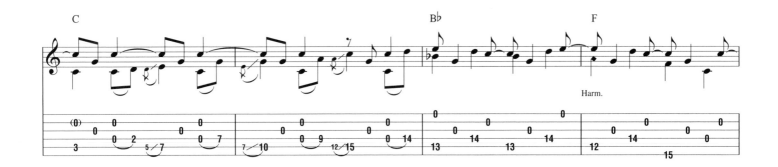

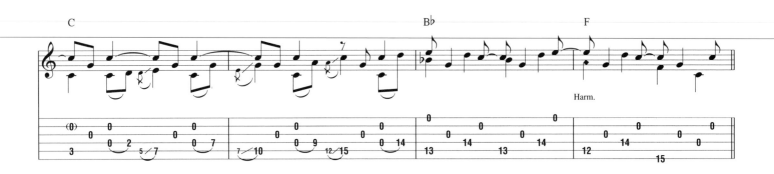

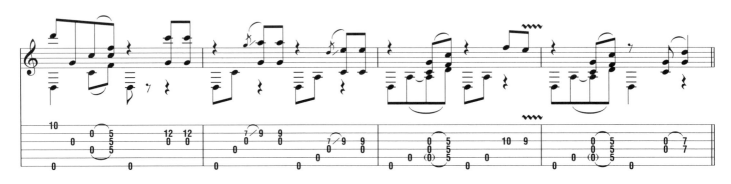

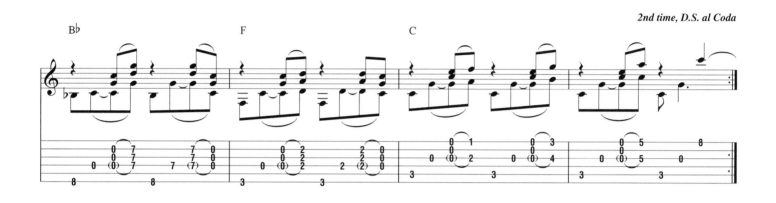

2nd time, D.S. al Coda

Coda

F

For Now

Music by Andy McKee

Tuning:
(low to high) C-G-D-F-B♭-D

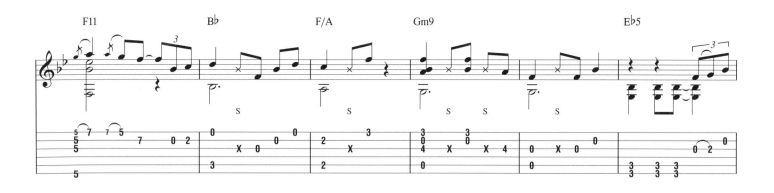

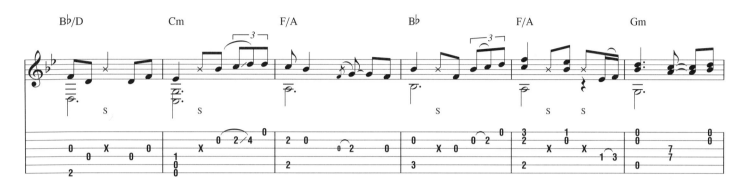

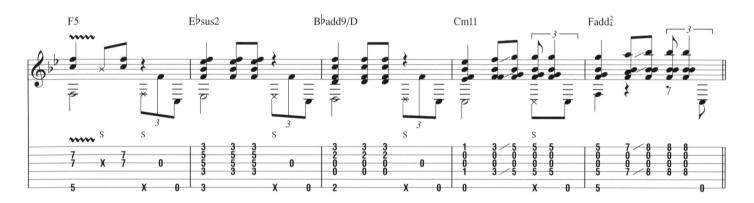

C

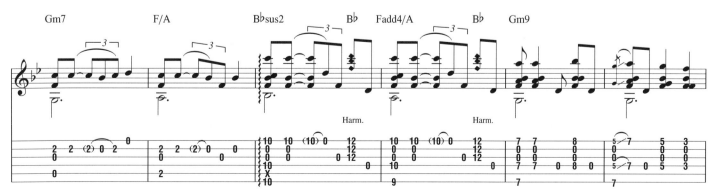

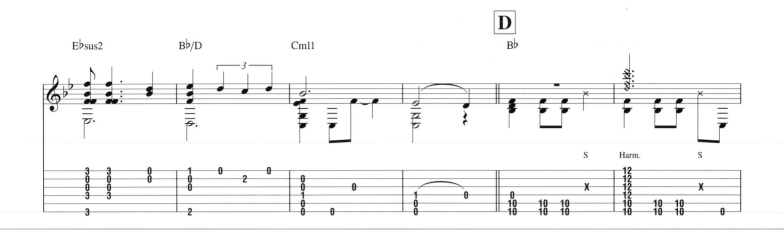

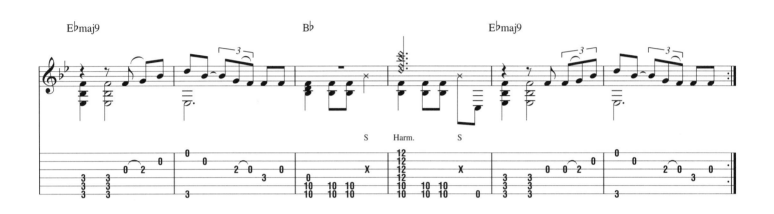

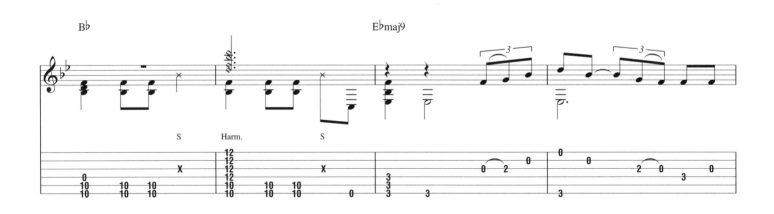

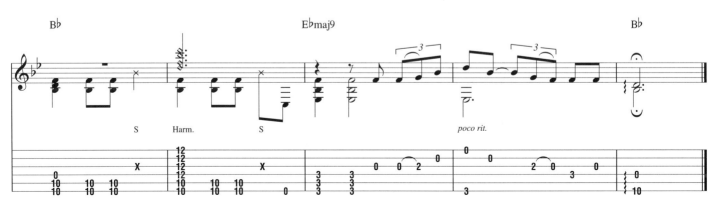